COMMUNITY WEBSITES

Published in the United States of America by Cherry Lake Publishing
Ann Arbor, Michigan
www.cherrylakepublishing.com

Content Advisor: Marcus Collins, MBA, Chief Consumer Connections Officer, Marketing Professor
Reading Adviser: Marla Conn MS, Ed., Literacy specialist, Read-Ability, Inc.

Photo Credits: © Rawpixel.com/Shutterstock.com, Cover, 1, 5; © Lenscap Photography/Shutterstock.com, 6; © Dragon Images/Shutterstock.com, 8; © photobyphotoboy/Shutterstock.com, 11; © chrisdorney/Shutterstock.com, 12; © Odua Images/Shutterstock.com, 15; © OlegKovalevichh/Shutterstock.com, pg 16; © Wagner Okasaki/Shutterstock.com, 19; © National Coalition Against Censorship/flickr, 20; © TijanaM/Shutterstock.com, 22; © G Holland/Shutterstock.com, 25; © peampath2812/Shutterstock.com, 26; © YAKOBCHUK VIACHESLAV/Shutterstock.com, 28

Library of Congress Cataloging-in-Publication Data

Names: Orr, Tamra, author.
Title: Community websites / Tamra B. Orr.
Description: [Ann Arbor, MI] : Cherry Lake Publishing, [2019] | Series: Global citizens : social media | Includes bibliographical
    references and index. | Audience: Grade 4 to 6.
Identifiers: LCCN 2018035589 | ISBN 9781534143074 (hardcover) | ISBN 9781534139633 (pbk.) | ISBN 9781534140837 (pdf) |
    ISBN 9781534142039 (hosted ebook)
Subjects: LCSH: History—Computer network resources—Juvenile literature. | Online social networks—Juvenile literature. |
    Internet—Social aspects—Juvenile literature.
Classification: LCC D16.117 .O77 2019 | DDC 025.06/307—dc23
LC record available at https://lccn.loc.gov/2018035589

Cherry Lake Publishing would like to acknowledge the work of the Partnership for 21st Century Learning.
Please visit www.p21.org for more information.

Printed in the United States of America
Corporate Graphics

ABOUT THE AUTHOR

Tamra Orr is the author of more than 500 nonfiction books for readers of all ages. A graduate of Ball State University, she now lives in the Pacific Northwest with her family. When she isn't writing books, she is either camping, reading, or on the computer researching the latest topic.

TABLE OF CONTENTS

CHAPTER 1
History: Becoming One of Us................................ 4

CHAPTER 2
Geography: Friends without Borders 10

CHAPTER 3
Civics: To Censor or Not to Censor? 18

CHAPTER 4
Economics: An Online Presence 24

THINK ABOUT IT... 30
FOR MORE INFORMATION..................................31
GLOSSARY 32
INDEX 32

History: Becoming One of Us

Have you ever had an important question but could not figure out the right person to ask? Have you wanted to share your passion for pugs, Korean pop, origami, fantasy sports, or a million other topics with someone who totally "gets it"?

Imagine reaching out to thousands of people who can help with these needs. You can do just that by exploring the almost infinite number of community sites (also known as **virtual** communities) available online. Community sites are places in which a group of individuals share and pursue common goals, feelings, and ideas through their interactions.

Before the internet, building a close-knit community was based on distance.

Many of these websites are **anonymous**. Unlike Facebook, for example, your comments and discussions are not connected to you and your profile (unless you make it known). This means you can discuss whatever you want without worrying what your friends or family will think. You can chat with people who may get you, but do not necessarily live in your city—or even your country.

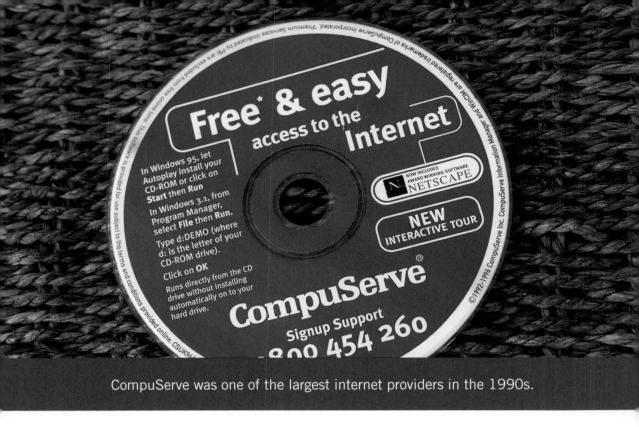

CompuServe was one of the largest internet providers in the 1990s.

From Chat Rooms to Communities

The very first online communities were born as chat rooms and email discussion lists during the 1980s, thanks to companies like CompuServe and America Online (AOL). Local people and hobbyists began chatting over specific bulletin board systems, posting on **forums** and sharing files. Multiplayer games quickly followed, with gamers able to not only conquer monsters and dungeons together, but also chat while doing so. By the early 2000s, many of these sites had evolved into social networks like Facebook and Myspace. From there, anonymous and gaming communities, like Reddit and Neopets, soon launched. These forums and sites united people with similar interests and created a sense of friendship between them.

Regardless of what type of online community people join, their ultimate goals are usually the same: to build relationships, share their common interests, and learn more about a specific topic. In today's world, there are plenty of choices!

Developing Questions

Do you belong to any online communities? If so, which ones and why did you join them? What kind of online community would you like to see or become a part of? Write down the topics you would like to discuss. Then look online to see if you find anything that fits those ideas. If not, explore what it might take to either create a separate forum on an existing website or create your own site.

Some online communities meet up in real life.

Types of Online Communities

Social   These are the most popular types of online communities. People generally talk, vent, and ask questions.

Support   These sites are designed for people looking for emotional or mental support for dealing with anything from health problems to changing circumstances.

Advocate or Action   These sites focus on campaigning for social change. They educate people on an important current topic and motivate them to get involved and do something about it.

Professional   People go to these communities to exchange information about a type of career, often asking or offering advice or sharing experiences. These are frequently used for **networking** as well.

Local   These are communities of people who live in the same neighborhood or area. They might be asking for recommendations for a good plumber, warning residents of upcoming road work, or asking for help in finding a lost dog.

Interest   These sites are based on a specific passion, hobby, or skill. People often exchange tips and ideas. These sites help people explore topics more deeply.

CHAPTER 2

Geography: Friends without Borders

Within seconds, you can be connected to countless people all over the world who have something in common with you. You can discuss anything you want, ask a question, get some advice, or simply share some ideas. Online communities are like having a group of friends around at all times in all places.

Two Online Giants

One of the best parts of virtual communities is that they have no borders or boundaries. You can talk to people in most parts of the world with just a few clicks of the mouse. Two of the biggest online communities are Pinterest and Reddit. Each site is unique, with hundreds of **subsets** and offshoots. They attract millions of regular users every month from all over the world.

As of January 2018, there were about 100 million Pinterest users outside the United States!

Pin It

Referred to as a visual bookmarking site, Pinterest has multiple categories, including art, crafts, fashion, food, science, travel, and DIY (do-it-yourself). When users find an interesting image, they can "pin" it to their "pinboard" for later reference or to share with others. Clicking on the image takes a person back to the original source. That delicious-looking pie probably links to the recipe. A photo of a ferret might link to a veterinarian's home page about caring for these animals.

In 2014, Massachusetts Institute of Technology (MIT) offered a course on Reddit.

Pinterest launched in 2010 and within 6 years, had more than 100 million active users. In 2014, Pinterest's international users grew an astounding 135 percent. By 2018, that number hit 200 million, with over 50 percent from outside the United States! The top four countries that pin, besides the United States, are Brazil, India, Russia, and Turkey.

r/Reddit

The other giant of online communities is Reddit. Launched in 2005 and known as the "front page of the internet," Reddit updates constantly and allows its users to anonymously discuss, respond, and interact with the news. Each individual community on Reddit is known as a subreddit, which begins with "r/" followed by the community name. Subreddits are like forums. They have their own page, subject matter, users, and **moderators**. Users post stories, links, images, videos, and other media to a community. Users then

Top Virtual Communities across the Globe

Webkinz	*Canadian social gaming community*
KASKUS	*Indonesian forum*
Habbo	*Finnish social gaming community*
Nairaland	*Nigerian forum*

Gathering and Evaluating Sources

It has become very important in today's culture to avoid gender **stereotyping**. *Deciding blue is for boys and pink is for girls is outdated. Look at the data below from Statista. What do men and women look at most on Pinterest? Does this support or not support cultural stereotypes? What do you find the most surprising about these numbers?*

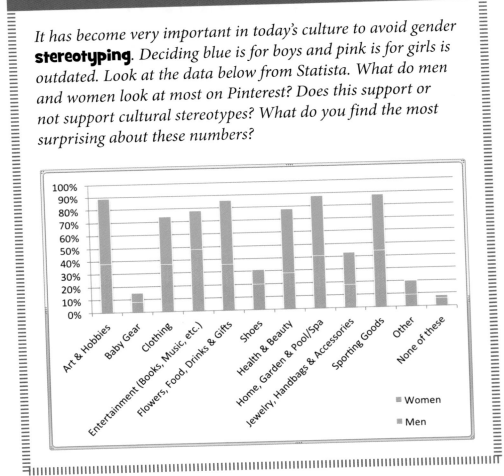

Favful is an online beauty community based in Southeast Asia.

vote and comment on them. The more votes a post gets, the higher it rises to the top of that community's page. Millions of comments are posted, and billions of pages are viewed every year.

As of mid-2018, Reddit is the seventh most popular website in the world. It's most popular in the United States, but close to half of the visitors (44 percent) are from countries all over the world. The United Kingdom and Canada follow the United States in having the most Reddit users.

Commenting anonymously online in China and Kazakhstan is illegal.
In fact, Kazakhstan websites will be fined over $700 if they don't comply.

Offline

In some countries, almost nothing is known about online community sites. In places like North Korea, China, India, Turkey, Iran, and Vietnam, various parts of the internet are constantly being banned. In China, millions of people have jobs as internet censors. North Korea has banned the entire internet—nothing is uploaded, downloaded, or viewed online. Only those with special government permission are able to access the internet.

Community sites may be made up of individuals, but together those millions of people are changing the way we meet, communicate, and interact. People no longer have to feel alone, because the whole world is out there just waiting to connect.

Civics: To Censor or Not to Censor?

Being able to remain anonymous on virtual communities gives users a great deal of freedom to be honest and say what they really feel. After all, the First Amendment guarantees everyone (including people online) the right to free speech. Right?

Reddit Censorship

Should people be able to say absolutely anything they want to? What if those words are hurtful or biased? Some community sites have had to face this issue and then deal with the consequences from their users. It is not easy. Many people believe **censorship** is wrong and refuse to be a part of community sites that limit what people can talk about. For example, Reddit had a subreddit that

The up and down arrows on Reddit, or upvotes and downvotes, were originally going to be "interesting" and "boring."

focused on mocking people who were overweight. It had thousands of members. The company decided to take it down, along with several others that shamed people for their race or gender identity. Many applauded Reddit's decision. But others were very critical, stating that the website had no right to determine what topics could and could not be discussed.

The National Coalition Against Censorship (NCAC) works with many people, including students, teachers, librarians, and parents, to promote freedom of thought, expression, and speech in all forms.

Thousands of Helping Hands

Reddit has also been behind some wonderful social causes. For example, its Secret Santa program makes sure that children all over the world receive gifts during the holidays. In 2012 and 2013, it set Guinness World Records for the largest gift exchanges. More than 89,000 people from 160 different countries participated. Reddit users have also raised money to help others. In Kenya, a children's orphanage needed $2,000 to build a concrete wall for protection. The Reddit community raised more than $100,000.

[21ST CENTURY SKILLS LIBRARY]

Communications Decency Act

If someone is offended by something discussed in a virtual community and asks for the posts to be taken down, can they legally sue if the company does not cooperate? Not according to the 1996 Communications Decency Act. It states that online community providers have almost total **immunity** from being

Getting the (Up)votes

In 2012, President Barack Obama went on Reddit for an "Ask Me Anything" (AMA) interview. So many users participated that the community site struggled with outages. At the end of the session, he stated, "I want to thank everybody at Reddit for participating. This is an example of how technology and the internet can empower the sorts of conversations that strengthen our democracy."

In the past, Reddit has held AMA interviews with celebrities such as physicist Neil DeGrasse Tyson and talk show hosts Stephen Colbert and Jimmy Kimmel. Obama's appearance was one of the largest in the site's history. To date, the AMA has over 216,000 upvotes!

About 28 million Americans, or 26 percent of online users, have used the internet to deepen their relationship with a community in real life.

legally responsible for what their users post. On user-run sites like Pinterest and Reddit, it is up to the users to exercise control over content, not the website owners.

Controlling the internet is rarely possible. While community sites are responsible for encouraging, educating, and helping millions, they are not without flaws. Censorship is sometimes an answer, but many feel it is not the best solution.

Developing Claims and Using Evidence

Personal opinions can often be turned into claims if they are backed up with evidence. Neopets is a virtual pet game site that allows users to interact with each other through games, **guilds***, public discussion boards (Neoboards), and direct messaging (Neomail). Because the virtual pet game attracts a younger audience, the site censors certain words. In addition, links to and mentions of fansites, like the subreddit for Neopets on Reddit, are banned as well. If users don't abide by these rules, their accounts can be frozen. Do you think censoring words and websites is okay? Why? With an adult's help, use the internet and resources at the library to further research this topic. Use the evidence you find to support your claims.*

Economics: An Online Presence

Online communities cover virtually every topic in the world. With each passing year, more companies are realizing this and jumping in on the trend. It is rare to find any company, no matter the size, that does not have some kind of online presence. Businesses know that creating a community of current and future customers is the best way to market their products, send out information, build **brand awareness**, and reach a huge audience. They also use these sites to answer questions, provide quality customer service, and ask their most loyal customers for feedback and **testimonials**.

Reddit co-founders, Alexis Ohanian and Steve Huffman, sold the site to a big company when they were just 22 years old!

Connecting with Customers

By creating a community, businesses make their customers feel like they are important, they belong, and they are valued. It is a win-win situation. Companies interact with consumers and, in turn, consumers can learn about a company's products, services, and **perspectives** before making a decision to buy something. Sephora is a great example of a company that fosters community. In 2017, the beauty store launched Beauty Insider Community. The virtual community allows its members to

Quora, a question and answer site, builds an online community based on asking and answering questions. The company is said to be worth about $1.7 billion!

discover, recommend, share, and discuss beauty-related topics with each other. Members also have the ability to ask other members of the Beauty Insider Community questions during checkout using the Live Community Chat.

Mary Beth Laughton, Sephora's executive vice president of digital retail, said the Beauty Insider Community is about driving emotional connections on both a consumer and personal level. The community also helps Sephora "learn a lot about [the] clients and . . . better personalize their experience." Businesses want people active on their sites. Research supports the fact that customers who actively participate on these sites end up coming back more often and spending more money.

Active Online Communities

There are hundreds of articles online explaining to companies why they need to be marketing directly to online communities. Virtually all of the articles agree on one thing: an active online community is an important key to any business's success.

Taking Informed Action

Hubski, one of the many online communities, does not have explicit rules about what can and cannot be discussed on its pages. However, it does state, "The best comments are those that generate thoughtful, civil conversation. You don't have to agree with others, but be respectful. Good comments are not necessarily popular perspectives, but are well-supported ones. If you assert a strong opinion, try to back it up with facts or an insightful **rationale***." What are they saying? In what ways can your opinions on a sensitive topic be presented with "insightful rationale"? What rules do you think should be in place?*

Companies are tapping into online communities
to better understand their market.

Happy customers spread the word. Vanessa DiMauro, an expert on online communities and marketing, states, "If you listen to members, if you respond to the members, if you provide them with thoughtful leadership, they will amplify the message."

Through online communities, people have the chance to reach out, connect, and bond over shared ideas, passions, and opinions. For many people, these communities give them a sense of belonging found nowhere else. They help any individual feel less alone and more united.

Communicating Conclusions

Before you read this book, were you a member of an online community? Now that you know more, has this changed how you see these virtual communities? Do you think being anonymous online creates more or less pressure on what you share? Do you think it creates stronger bonds? Share your thoughts with your friends and family. Ask them what they think.

Think About It

Pinterest has had a huge impact on online shoppers' purchasing decisions. Two-thirds of the items people pin represent a specific brand or product. An estimated 47 percent of online shoppers in the United States, for example, have reported buying something solely based on a recommendation they saw on Pinterest. Even more importantly, 87 percent of active "pinners" report they have bought something because they saw it on this site. What do you think this data means about the future of shopping?

For More Information

FURTHER READING

Bernhardt, Carolyn. *Pin It! Pinterest Projects for the Real World.* Minneapolis: Checkerboard Library, 2017.

Krumsiek, Allison. *Cyber Mobs: Destructive Online Communities.* New York: Lucent Press, 2017.

Leavitt, Amie Jane. *Combatting Toxic Online Communities.* New York: Rosen Publishing, 2016.

Waters, Rosa. *Pinterest: How Ben Silbermann and Evan Sharp Changed the Way We Share What We Love.* Broomall, PA: Mason Crest, 2015.

Wheeler, Jill. *Pinterest.* Minneapolis: Checkerboard Library, 2017.

WEBSITES

Neopets
www.neopets.com
Keep your pet alive and chat with friends from all over the world while learning basic coding and economics.

Animal Jam
www.animaljam.com/welcome
Explore the outdoors as your favorite animal and chat with other users in this virtual world.

GLOSSARY

anonymous (uh-NAH-nuh-muhs) unknown or unidentified

brand awareness (BRAND uh-WAIR-nis) how familiar consumers are with a brand of goods or services

censorship (SEN-sur-ship) the practice of not publishing something that is considered offensive

forums (FOR-uhmz) online meeting places for discussions of various topics

guilds (GILDZ) groups of users with similar interests

immunity (ih-MYOON-uh-tee) protection from harm

moderators (MAH-duh-rate-urz) people who are in charge of discussions

networking (NET-wurk-ing) meeting people and sharing professional or social information with them

perspectives (pur-SPEK-tivz) attitudes toward or ways of looking at something

rationale (rah-shuh-NAHL) reason or explanation

stereotyping (STER-ee-oh-tipe-ing) reducing someone to a category based on only one element

subsets (SUHB-setz) groups of things that are part of a larger group

testimonials (tes-tuh-MOH-nee-uhlz) positive reports on the qualities of something

virtual (VUR-choo-uhl) made to seem like the real thing but actually coming from a computer

INDEX

America Online (AOL), 6
anonymity, 5, 7, 13, 16, 18, 29

businesses, 24–29

censorship, 18–23
chat rooms, 6–7
Communications Decency Act, 21, 23
community sites. *See* online communities
CompuServe, 6

economics, 24–29

Facebook, 5, 7
forums, 6, 7, 13
free speech, 18

gaming communities, 6–7, 13
geography, 10–17

Hubski, 27

Myspace, 7

Neopets, 7, 23

Obama, Barack, 21
online communities
   banned, 16, 17
   censorship, 18–23
   companies' uses for, 24–29
   economics, 24–29
   geography, 10–17
   history, 4–9
   most popular worldwide, 13
   statistics, 22
   types of, 9

Pinterest, 10, 11–12, 14, 23, 30

Quora, 26

Reddit, 7, 10, 12–15, 20, 21, 23, 25
   censorship, 18–19

Sephora, 25–26
social causes, 20
social networks, 7

virtual communities. *See* online communities